WHAT'S IN YOUR GRISLY GUTS?

Written by John Farndon

Illustrated by Alan Rowe

First published in 2023 by Hungry Tomato Ltd
F15, Old Bakery Studios, Blewetts Wharf, Malpas Road, Truro, Cornwall, TR1 1QH, UK.

A CIP catalogue record for this book is available from the British Library.

Published and Distributed in India by Scholastic India Pvt. Ltd.

ISBN 978-93-5954-367-3

This reprint edition : January 2025

Printed in India at Shree Maitrey Printech Pvt. Ltd., Noida

Discover more at
www.hungrytomato.com

CONTENTS

WHAT'S IN YOUR GUTS?

Your body is an incredible machine that can do all sorts of amazing things. Thanks to your body, you can enjoy eating tasty food.

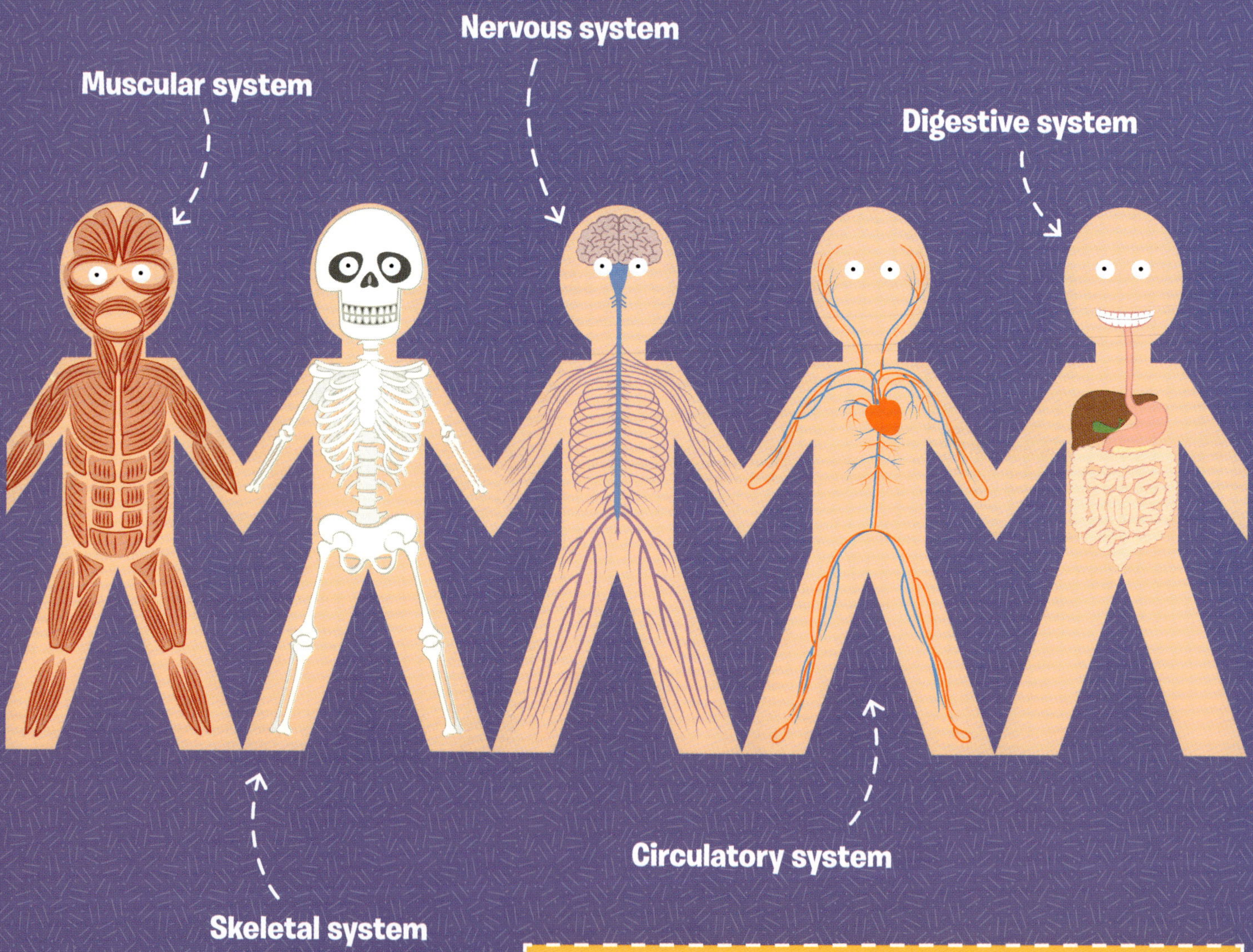

How does your body work?

Your body is all about teamwork. Different parts work together in teams, called systems, to perform different tasks.

Where does your food go?

Food travels through your body's food factory, the digestive system, where it goes through many changes. It starts in your mouth and ends in the toilet.

Let's find out more about why we need food and what happens on its amazing (and kind of gross) journey through your body.

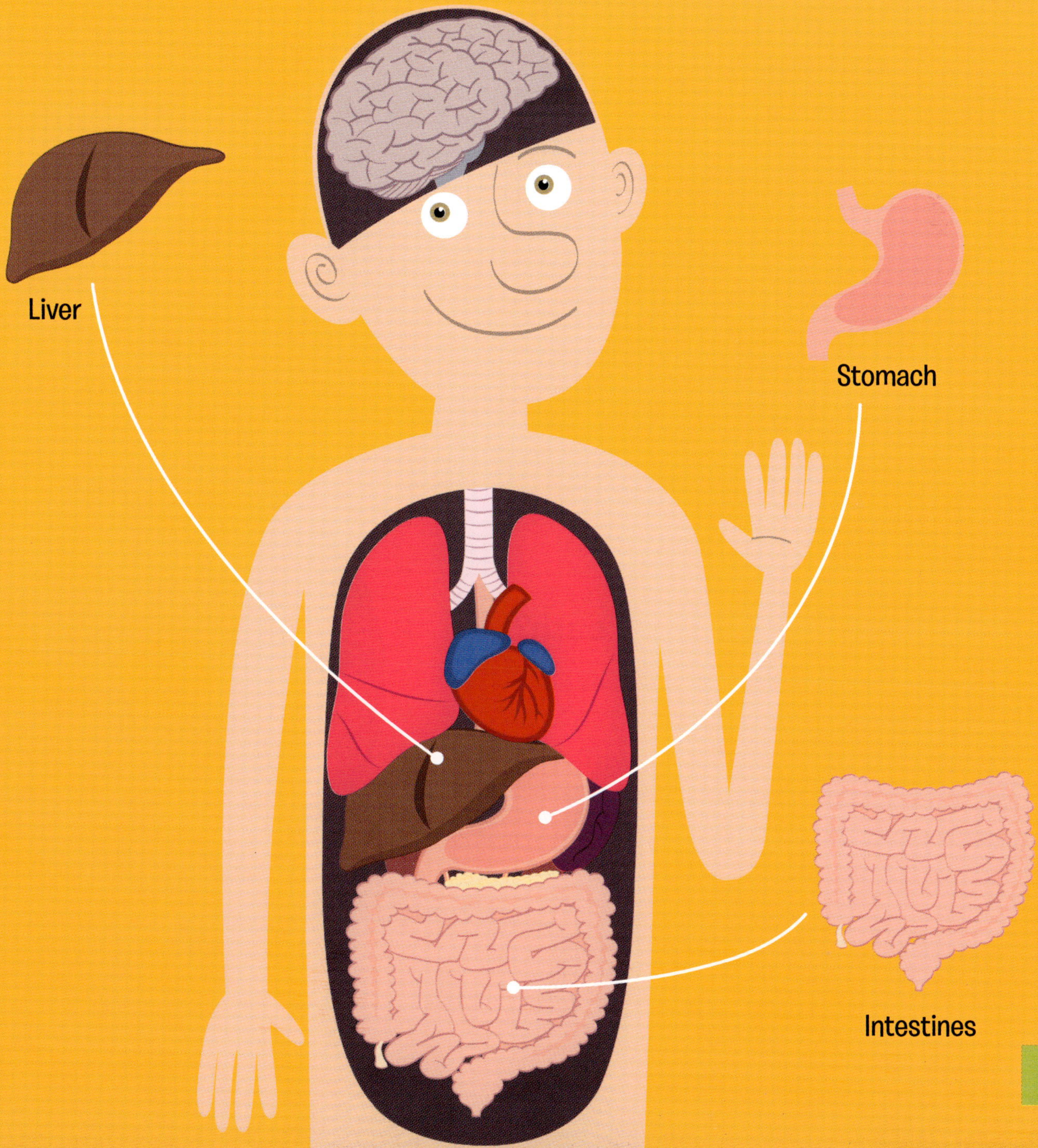

WHAT A MOUTHFUL!

Most of us just love stuffing our mouths with food. But just what goes on in there?

What do your teeth do?

Your food gets mashed to a pulp between your teeth. You have about 32 teeth, and each one has a coat of **enamel**, the body's toughest substance.

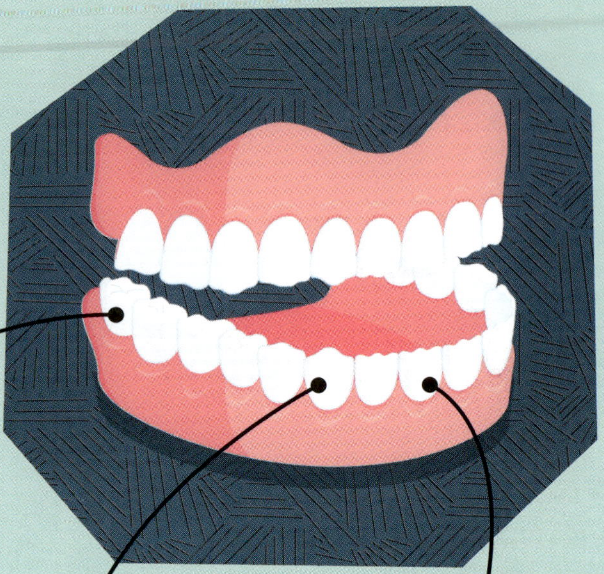

Molars

These teeth, at the back, are big crushers and mashers.

Canines

These teeth, at the side, are rippers.

Incisors

These teeth, at the front, are sharp choppers and slicers.

Why must we clean our teeth?

If you don't clean your teeth every day, they will soon be coated in a sticky goo called plaque, which contains a lot of **bacteria**. Yuck! These bacteria ooze chemicals that can rot your tooth enamel.

Why does yummy food make you drool?

Liquid saliva in your mouth helps soften food. When you smell something nice, your brain tells your salivary glands to start oozing saliva into your mouth.

Chemicals in saliva, called enzymes, help turn food mushy.

It also contains chemicals that heal cuts and look after your teeth.

GOT TO EAT

Food can be really yummy, but that's not the only reason we eat it.

What's food for?

Like filling a car with fuel, eating food gives you energy to move, and helps you stay warm. Food also gives stuff you need for growing and staying well.

Carbohydrates

Sugary and starchy foods are great energy fuel for your body.

Fats

Your body stores fat from food to use as emergency energy.

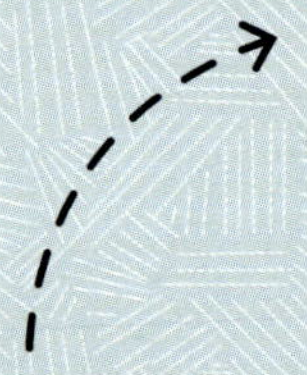

Protein

Most of your body is made from materials called proteins. But you can't make them all. That's why you need to eat foods with proteins to stay healthy.

What are vitamins and minerals?

Vitamins and minerals are super substances that are found in the food we eat. Different foods contain specific vitamins and minerals that help different parts of your body stay healthy.

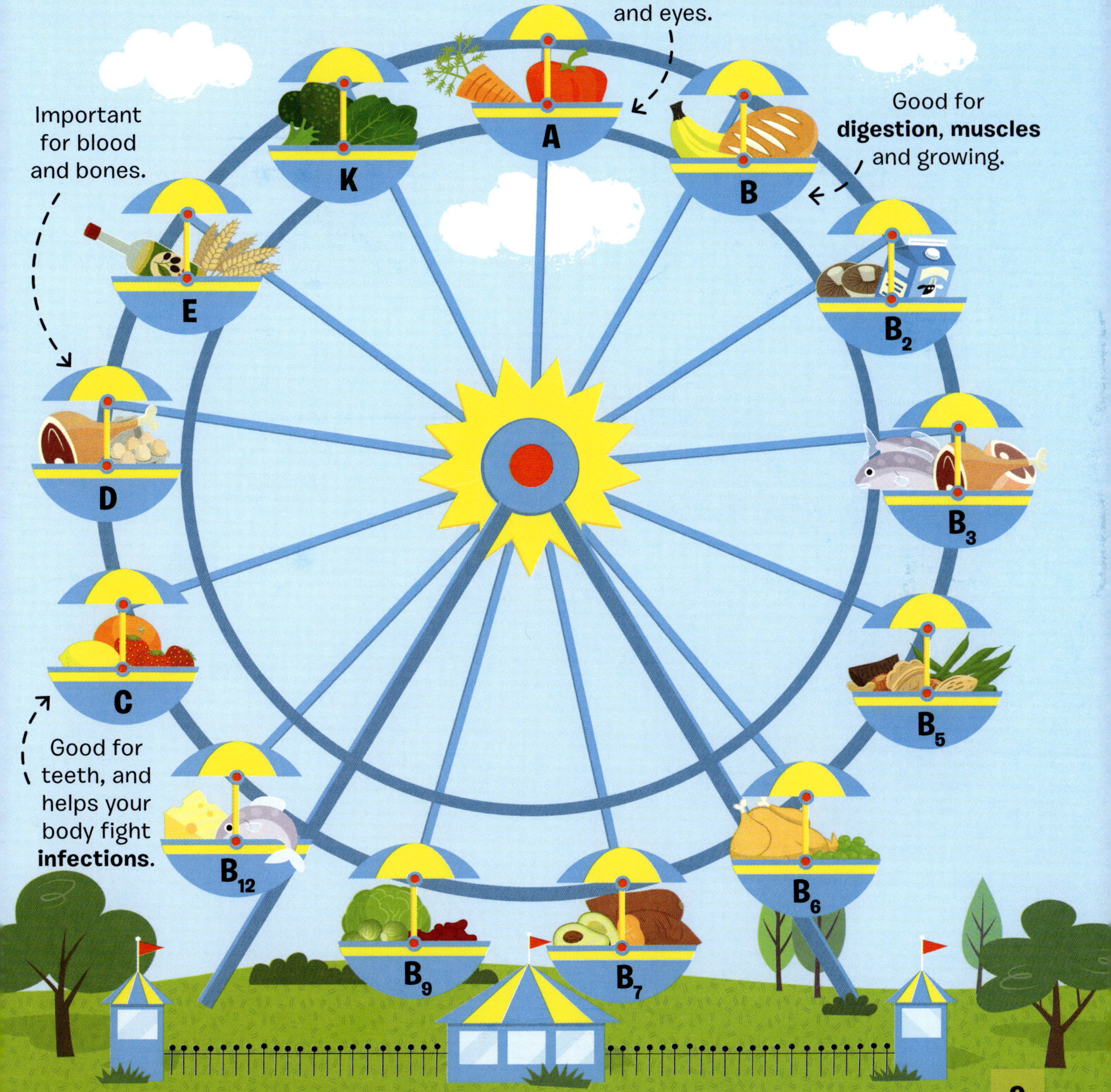

(Note: Vitamins are named with letters of the alphabet. But, just to confuse us all, there are a lot of different B vitamins.)

BELLY BUSINESS

Have you ever wondered what happens to your food after you've swallowed it?

Where does food go?

Down your throat and into your stomach. When it's empty, your stomach is tiny. But when food arrives, it swells up like a balloon.

What happens inside your stomach?

Your stomach (or tummy or belly) is a heavyweight food masher! Food is attacked in it with powerful juices and crushed to a pulp by squeezing muscles.

What's vomit?

Vomit is mushed-up food from your stomach, along with its slimy lining, saliva and stomach juices.

What makes you throw up?

If your stomach is upset, the "vomit spot" in your brain tells some stomach muscles to open and others to squeeze from below, then whoosh, up it comes through your mouth. Yuck!

Why do you burp?

Burps are the sounds you make when gas escapes from your stomach through your mouth. Every day, you burp enough gas to fill a one litre bottle.

YOU'VE GOT GUTS

We've all got guts, gurgling away inside us. That's where your food goes. But why do you need guts?

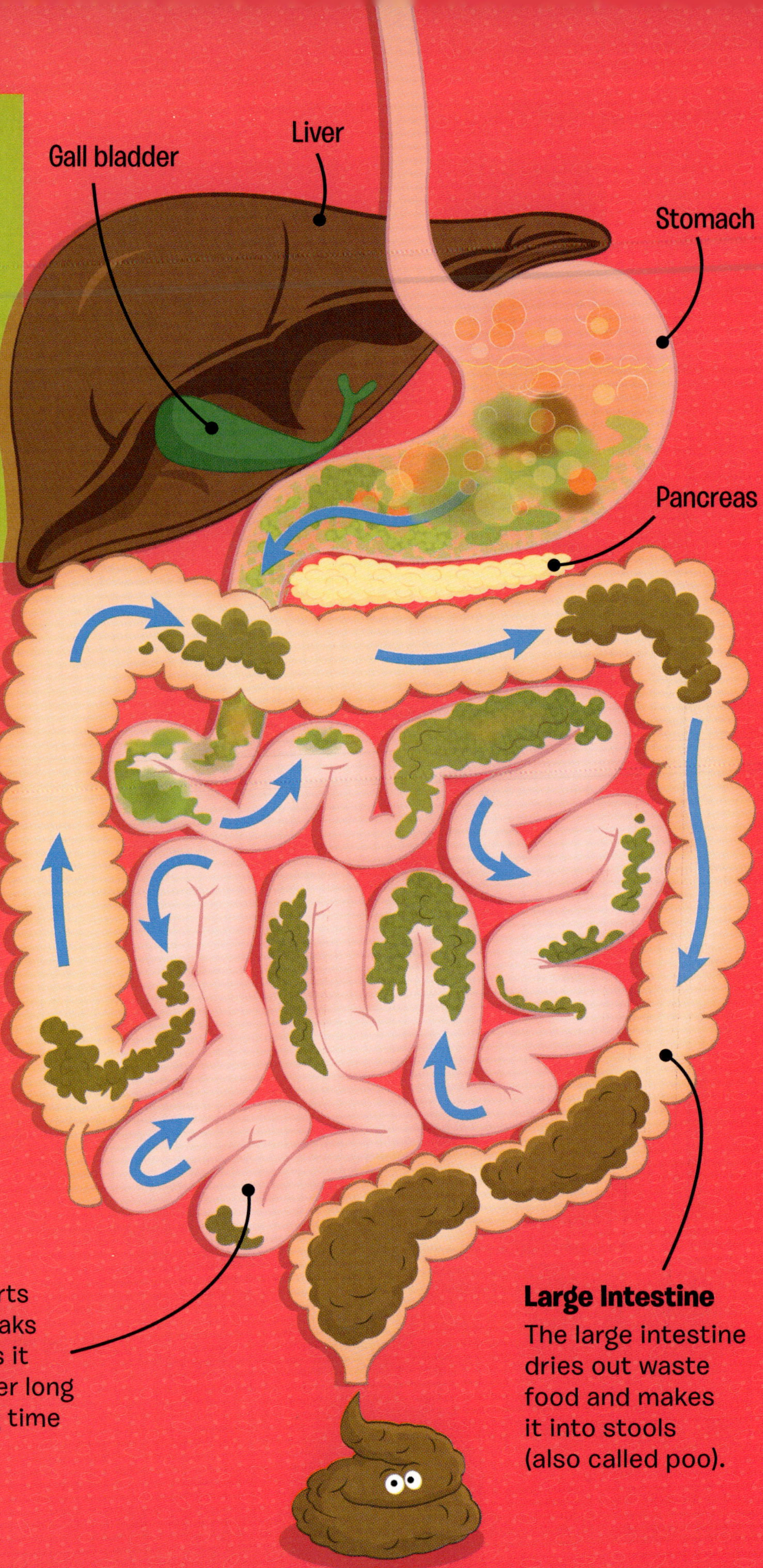

What are guts?

They're a super-long tunnel twisted around inside you, called the digestive tract. There's a thin part called the small intestine and a fat one called the large intestine.

Small Intestine

The small intestine starts at your stomach. It breaks down food and absorbs it into your body. It's super long because it takes a long time to break food down.

Large Intestine

The large intestine dries out waste food and makes it into stools (also called poo).

How long does it take food to travel through your body?

Food working its way through your body is called digestion. How long it takes depends on what you've eaten, but it's usually between 2 and 5 days.

It takes 8 seconds for food to get to your stomach.

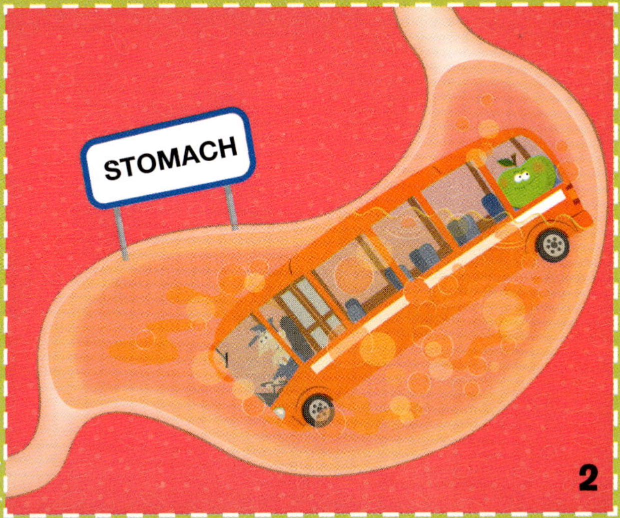

Food spends 2 to 4 hours in your stomach.

It takes 3 to 5 hours to get through your small intestine.

What's left in the large intestine can hang around for about 36 hours!

BUSY LIVER

Food is full of all kinds of useful ingredients. But how does your body get them working for you?

What does your liver do?

Your liver is your own personal factory for turning the useful ingredients that your intestines took from your food into substances your body can use.

1. It turns most of the sugars and starches from your food into glucose, your body's fuel.

Is that all your liver does?

No. Your liver is a super multitasker with a lot of jobs, including . . .

. . . making new liquid for your blood, called plasma . . .

. . . storing vitamins and minerals . . .

. . . making bile, a yellowish liquid that it sends to the intestines to help break down food . . .

. . . and that's just to start! It can even regrow itself! What a smart organ!

2. It also stores some as an emergency fuel supply, called glycogen.

3. It packages any leftovers into fat and sends it around your body.

BETTER OUT THAN IN!

Everyone uses the toilet and farts! But, have you ever wondered why?

Why do we poo?

Not everything in the food we eat can be used by the body. The leftover waste at the end of the digestion process comes out as stools (or faeces), which we call poo.

What's in a stool?

A stool contains:

Bacteria
Don't worry, these are good bacteria that help with digestion and keep you healthy.

Water

Bile
A yellow liquid made in the liver that breaks down fat.

Fibre
Foods have fibre that can help food move smoothly through the digestive system, but it doesn't break down itself.

What is a fart?

A fart is a mixture of gases that form as your food breaks down inside you. These gases need to go somewhere, so they come out as smelly farts!

Why do they smell bad?

Some gases have a scent. The different gases that form a fart can be pretty smelly when they are combined together!

WHEN YOU'VE GOT TO GO . . .

We all have to pee a few times a day, sometimes at very awkward moments. What's that all about?

What's in your pee?

The proper name for pee is urine. It is mostly water, but small amounts of other things get flushed out with it.

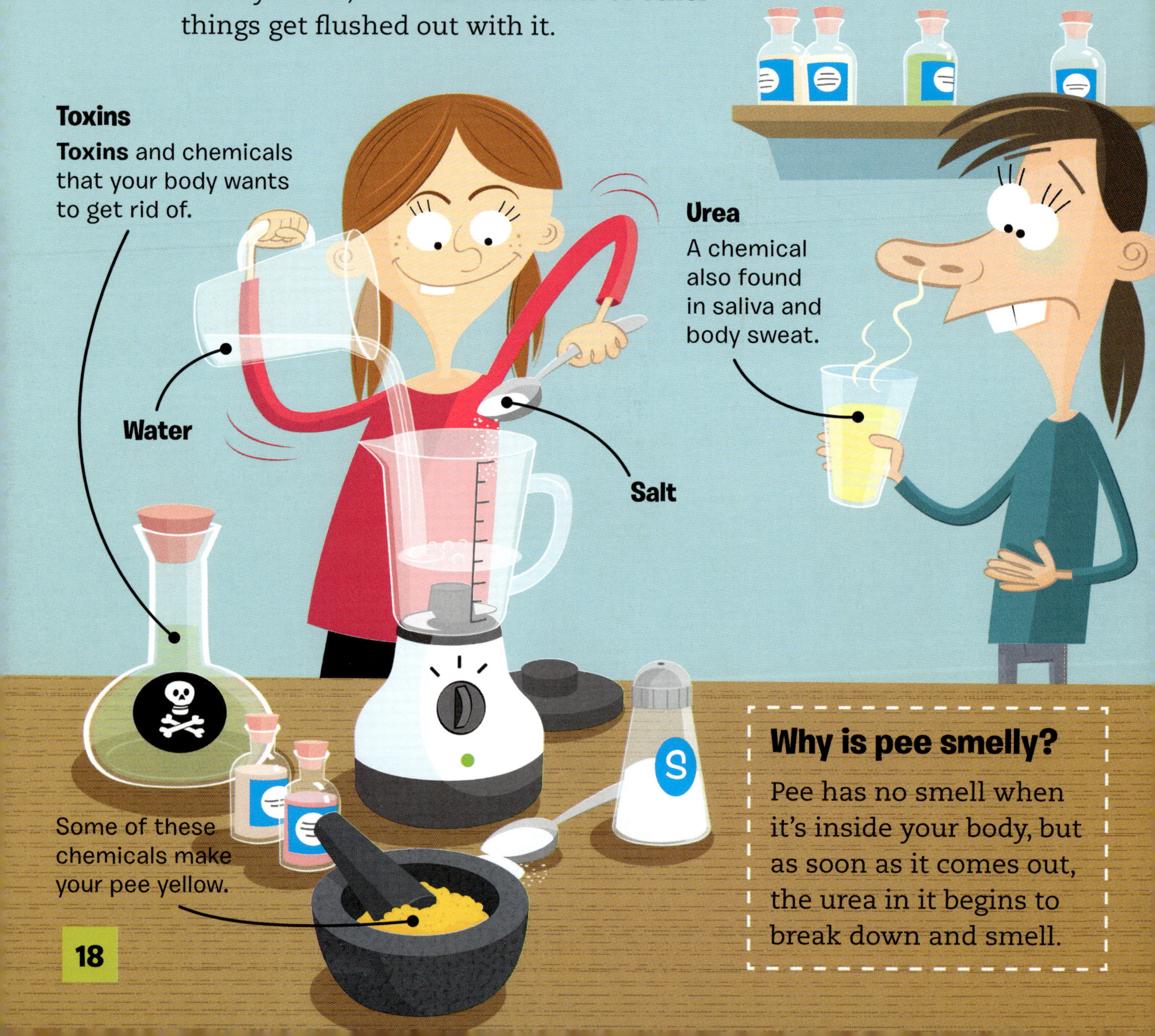

Why is pee smelly?

Pee has no smell when it's inside your body, but as soon as it comes out, the urea in it begins to break down and smell.

Why do we pee?

You take in water all the time by eating and drinking. So, you have to pee to keep the amount of water in your body just right.

Why does water matter?

Your body is mostly made of water. It's amazing you don't slosh around when you walk! You need to drink plenty of water to keep everything in your body working properly.

HOT STUFF

Your body is like a little heater, which is why your bed feels warm in the morning. So, why are we warm?

How do you keep warm?

Your body's heat comes from the food you eat. Your liver and body **cells** are like little stoves turning the energy stored in sugar into heat. Putting on extra clothes helps, too!

How do you keep cool?

You keep cool mostly by breathing out. That's why your breath is warm. You also lose heat through your skin, which is why you wear less clothes in hot weather. Sweating helps, too!

Why's your body hot?

Cakes need to be cooked at the right temperature to bake well, right? Well, your body has to stay at the right temperature to work properly, too. Around 37°C (98.6°F) is perfect.

If it gets too hot or too cold, you get ill.

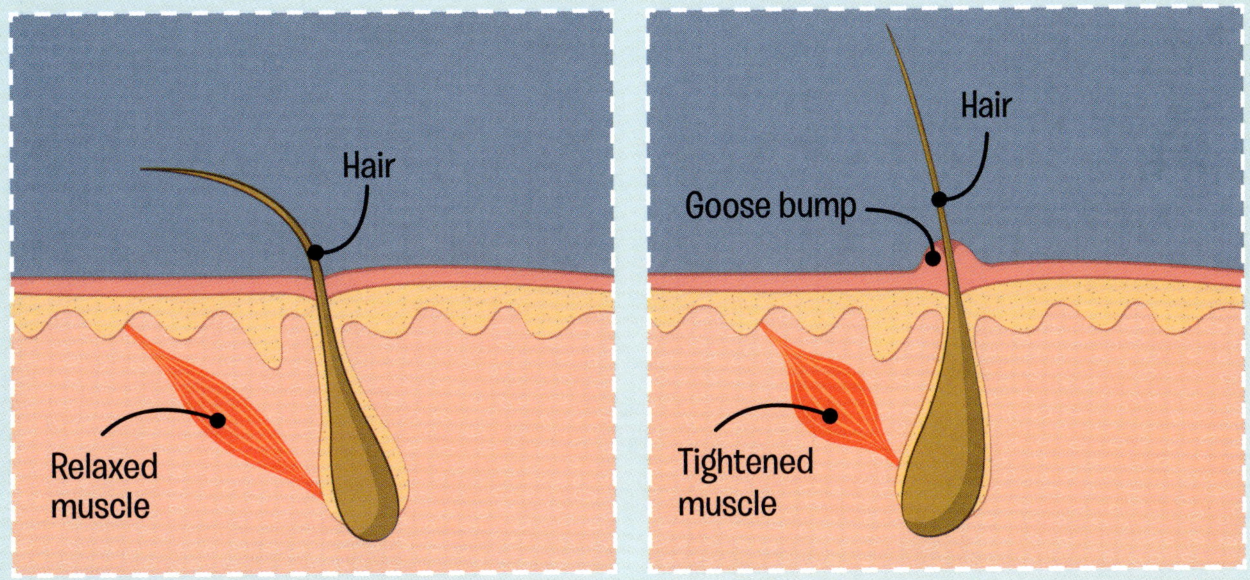

What are goosebumps?

When you're cold, your skin may get goosebumps. These happen when little muscles under your skin make your hairs stand up to try and trap a layer of warm air, like furry animals do.

GLOSSARY

bacteria
Tiny living things made from just one cell.

cells
Our bodies are made up of trillions of tiny, squishy packages, called cells. We have lots of different types of cells for each body part.

digestion
The process of breaking down food in your body.

enamel (tooth)
A hard, smooth substance that covers and protects your teeth.

infections
When germs invade your body and cause it harm.

muscles
Muscles are bundles of rope-like tissue that tighten and relax to make your body move. You have more that 650 muscles all over your body.

toxins
Poisonous substances created by living things.

INDEX

About the Author

John Farndon is the author of a huge number of books for adults and children on science, history and nature, including international bestsellers, *Do Not Open* and *Do You Think You're Clever?*. He has been shortlisted for the Young People's Science Book Prize five times, including for the book *Project Body*.

About the Illustrator

Alan Rowe has been working as a freelance Illustrator since 1985. His work is heavily influenced by 1950s and 60s cartoons. Maybe all that time spent glued to the TV as a child wasn't all wasted!